Original title:
Peachy Moments

Copyright © 2025 Creative Arts Management OÜ
All rights reserved.

Author: Nathaniel Blackwood
ISBN HARDBACK: 978-1-80586-234-5
ISBN PAPERBACK: 978-1-80586-706-7

Tranquil Medleys of Sweet Memories

In the orchard's gentle sway,
Laughter dances, bright and gay,
Forgotten hats and sticky hands,
Nature's joy, it understands.

Silly faces, fruit-filled fights,
Squeezed between the sunny bites,
A splash of juice, a cheerful grin,
Who knew this mess would spark such sin?

Chasing shadows, soft and sweet,
Bouncing balls and happy feet,
Giggles echo in the trees,
Tucked away in memories' breeze.

From tree to swing, a merry ride,
Beneath the sun, with friends beside,
Each folly stored like treasure bright,
In hearts that dance with sheer delight.

Sweet Nostalgia in Each Squeeze

Juicy laughter in every bite,
Memories sticky, oh what a sight.
Childhood summers dripping sweet,
Giggling friends we'd often meet.

Chasing shadows, feeling bold,
A treasure chest of stories told.
Popsicles melting in the sun,
Life's little moments, oh what fun!

A Dance of Colors on My Tongue

Cotton candy clouds and bright delights,
Swirling rainbows, bold in the sights.
Candy hues like laughter's song,
Each flavor a memory, soft and strong.

Bouncing bites, a carnival cheer,
With every taste, it all feels near.
Lemon drops and cherry spins,
In every ring, a giggle wins.

Radiance in the Shade of Trees

Under branches, we played so free,
Sipping sunshine, just you and me.
Memory lane paved with bright smiles,
We danced and sang, stretching for miles.

Glimmers of joy, where shadows play,
Summers linger, brightening the day.
Whispers of laughter, the breeze does bring,
Echoing softly, sweet notes to sing.

Golden Days and Melting Hearts

Chocolate smiles and sticky hands,
Little moments like magic bands.
Running wild, the world our stage,
Every laugh, a turning page.

Golden sunsets, a perfect end,
Each bite a hug from a dear friend.
Silly stories float in the air,
Life's little gifts, beyond compare.

The Glow of Tender Memories

A fuzzy fruit rests on my plate,
Its soft skin tempting, oh what a fate!
I take a bite, the juice does spurt,
Dripping on my shirt, oh what a flirt!

Laughter erupts as I try to clean,
A sight so silly, a sticky sheen.
Friends point and giggle at the mess I've made,
In this fruity chaos, we've got it made.

A Dance of Juicy Moments

Twirl around the kitchen, it's quite the affair,
With fruit in hand, I dance without care.
Slicing and dicing, what a fun sight,
Yet somehow the juice goes flying with might!

Lemon, peach, and a splash of zest,
A comedy show, we're all quite blessed.
Caught up in laughter, we jump and slide,
As snacks turn to puddles, we can't hide.

Whimsical Flavors of the Afternoon

Sippin' on smoothies, each flavor a tease,
A swirl of colors, oh what a breeze!
Giggling together, sipping too fast,
The chaos erupts with each giggly blast!

We build a fruit tower that stretches so high,
Then watch it topple, oh me, oh my!
Laughter erupts, as we scramble to wield,
The pieces of joy from our fruity field.

Flush of Delight Beneath Bright Skies

Under the sun, we bask with glee,
Plump juicy fruits, a sight to see.
Watermelons wobble, cherries laugh bright,
We toss them around, oh what a sight!

With each little splash, our joy starts to bloom,
Dancing with fruit as we fill up the room.
Sticky hands and faces, a mess of pure cheer,
In these silly moments, we hold each dear.

Timeless Moments Woven with Gold

In a park where giggles roam,
Silly hats like mushrooms bloom.
Ice cream drips on sunny hands,
Laughter echoes, happiness expands.

Bubbles float like dreams on air,
Chasing them, we do not care.
Squirrels dance with silly flair,
Life's a circus, full of dare.

Friends play tag on grassy hills,
Voices clash like joyful thrills.
Fortune cookies tell us lies,
But we laugh 'til we cry.

Effervescent Joy in Every Shade

Soda fizzing, laughter spills,
Rainbow sprinkles give us chills.
Kites take flight, a goofy chase,
Giggles painted on each face.

Water balloons in playful fight,
Splashes glow in the warm sunlight.
Silly faces, chalk on skin,
Every moment, a joyful win.

Dance like no one's watching near,
In the chaos, joy appears.
Every shade of funny glee,
Life's a canvas, wild and free.

A Mosaic of Flavorful Sunshine

Cupcakes spinning, colorful stars,
Whipped cream clouds dance on our jars.
Taste-testing every silly snack,
Chasing flavors, we won't look back.

Pickles dipped in chocolate dreams,
Popcorn rains fall in playful streams.
Silly straws that twist and bend,
Each silly sip, a brand-new trend.

Lemonade spills in giddy glee,
Fighting over who can drink free.
Sweet and sour, we laugh and sigh,
Mosaic moments, oh my, oh my!

Enchanted Travels Through Sweet Serenity

In a van with seats so small,
Singing tunes, we barely stall.
Roadtrips filled with quirky sights,
Freestyling through the starry nights.

Maps are tattered, plans are loose,
Every turn, a chance to cruise.
Finding treasures, hidden gems,
A giggling crew, life's happy stems.

Frozen yogurt, we take a break,
With sprinkles on our road-trip cake.
Chasing sunsets, laughing wide,
These sweet journeys, joy can't hide.

Laughter Floating on Warm Breezes

The sun spills giggles on the grass,
Children chase shadows, a wild dance.
Ice cream drips from sticky hands,
As laughter twirls through summer's trance.

Glimmers of joy in each bright smile,
A dog chases squirrels, full of glee.
The air is thick with playful jest,
As we roll down hills, carefree and free.

Ripened Joy in Every Bite

Juicy smiles break on a slice,
Fruity flavors burst like jokes.
A single bite, a silly noise,
As sticky hands become the folk.

We munch on sweetness, laughter shares,
With each crisp crunch, the world feels bright.
Spilling juice on clothes and pride,
A messy feast feels just so right.

Orchard Secrets and Sun-Kissed Tales

In shady groves where secrets hide,
We sneak the best fruits in a race.
The whispers of trees share joyful lore,
While we take turns with our silly grace.

A basket fills with giggles too,
As ripe fruits tumble, laughter flows.
We dance beneath the buzzing bees,
Telling tales only youth knows.

The Harmony of Heat and Flavor

Sun-soaked afternoons invite a feast,
As flavors mingle in a light breeze.
The heat sparks laughter just like fire,
With each delightful bite, we're at ease.

Sips of sweet nectar, laughter swells,
We share the warmth that summer gives.
With every taste, our hearts take flight,
In joyful chaos, we truly live.

A Radiant Dance of Flavors

In a bowl of bright delight,
Fruits collide, oh what a sight!
Juicy whispers in the sun,
Taste the laughter, oh what fun!

Grapes sneak in a merry dance,
To the beat of summer's chance.
Oranges giggle, ripe and round,
Sweetest joy is what we've found!

With a spritz of zesty cheer,
Every moment, so sincere.
In this kitchen, joy abounds,
Flavor's magic knows no bounds!

Splashing Joy in Sunny Puddles

Splashing colors everywhere,
Water fights without a care.
Rubber ducks and silly screams,
Summer days burst into dreams!

Sprinklers dance in wild delight,
Chasing shadows, what a sight!
Children giggle, run, and glide,
In the sun, they take a ride!

Wet grass tickles tiny toes,
So much fun, where joy just flows.
A splash of dreams, a gentle cheer,
Sunny puddles, hold me near!

Golden Melodies of Exuberant Days

Banjos twang as laughter soars,
Sunshine spills through open doors.
Cookies crumble, hugs abound,
Joyful music all around!

Through the air, sweet notes will play,
Twirling memories every day.
Silly dances, big and wide,
In this moment, hearts collide!

Chasing dreams on rainbow trails,
Every giggle never fails.
Together humming life's sweet song,
In this magic, we belong!

Lush Gardens of Laughter and Light

In gardens bright, the fun's alive,
Bouncing bunnies, joy will thrive.
Flowers wink and wink in glee,
Playful shades of harmony!

Butterflies with wiggly flight,
Twirl and sway, oh what a sight!
Tickled petals, laughter spritz,
In this play, the heart just fits!

Sunbeams dance on dewy grass,
Time stands still, as moments pass.
Nature's joke, a cosmic laugh,
In this bliss, we find our path!

Caramel Sunsets and Sweet Escapes

The sun dips low with a grin,
Marshmallow clouds begin to spin.
Squirrels dance with vibrant flair,
Catching dreams in the evening air.

Joy spills out like melted fudge,
While the crickets softly trudge.
A hammock sways, a laughter shared,
Underneath a sky that dared.

Fireflies flash like tiny stars,
As we laugh and raise our jars.
With lemonade, we toast the night,
Watching shadows play in light.

Caramel dreams on the horizon,
With every giggle, we're risin'.
Nature's humor, bold and bright,
We bask in love's sweet, silly sight.

Harmony in Nature's Bounty

Birds are playing hide and seek,
While ants march with tiny squeaks.
Flowers whisper silly jokes,
As butterflies flash by like folks.

The breeze giggles in your ear,
As the trees sway without fear.
Berries burst with fruity glee,
Nature's bounty, wild and free.

A frog croaks in a burly style,
While rabbits watch and then compile.
Every step is full of cheer,
In this wild place, we draw near.

Laughter bubbles in streams near,
As we soak in all the cheer.
With nature's gifts, we intertwine,
In giggles, life's best sign.

Golden Rhapsody of Life's Delight

A squirrel wears a tiny hat,
As he scampers past a sleeping cat.
Sunshine tickles toes so bare,
Every moment catches air.

The butterflies throw a grand ball,
Inviting us to dance, oh what a call!
With petals floating all around,
We twirl and laugh—what joy we've found.

Picnic spreads with treats galore,
As ants waltz up for a score.
Each juicy bite brings pure delight,
As giggles float into the night.

Golden glimmers paint the sky,
With every wink, the day slips by.
Sweet moments spiral, loop, and twine,
In this rhapsody, we shine.

Laughter Laced with Summer's Perfume

A watermelon hat sits askew,
As we splash in a pool so blue.
Lemonade dribbles down our chins,
With sticky fingers, summer wins.

The sun winks with a bright golden eye,
As friends chase clouds that drift on by.
Every jump brings squeals of glee,
Underneath the old oak tree.

Marshmallows roast, some fall on toes,
Bonfire laughter, anything goes.
Stories told with silly grins,
As starlit nights begin to spin.

With each giggle, the fire glows,
In summer evenings, pure joy flows.
A fragrant breeze that wraps us tight,
In laced laughter, our hearts take flight.

A Tapestry of Sunkissed Dreams

Under the sun, we giggle loud,
Chasing shadows in a cheerful crowd.
Ice cream drips on a funny hat,
Laughter swirls like a playful cat.

We dance on grass, our feet so free,
With every twirl, we squeal with glee.
Silly poses for the camera flash,
Creating memories in a joyful bash.

The breeze sings tunes of mischief bright,
As we leap and stumble with pure delight.
Sun-kissed cheeks with freckles bloom,
We embrace the carefree afternoon.

In this tapestry of joyful cream,
We weave our stories, thread by theme.
With every stitch, a laughter flows,
Beneath the sun, where happiness grows.

Radiant Reflections in Ripe Harmony

Bouncing berries on a picnic spread,
I thought I saw a butterfly's head.
A squirrel watched, eyes wide and round,
As I tripped over my own two bound.

Giggles echo in the summer heat,
As we challenge each other with funny feet.
Cakes are dropped, frosting flies high,
It's a dessert war, oh me, oh my!

We toast with lemonade, icy and sweet,
Mixing laughter as our voices meet.
With every sip, a story spins,
Reflecting joy where the fun begins.

As dusk approaches, we dance with flair,
The twilight air seems to stutter and stare.
In moments ripe, let the laughter grow,
A harmony of joy, stealing the show.

Echoes of Happiness at Dusk

The sky turns pink as we make a pact,
To unearth treasures in laughter intact.
With fireflies buzzing, we play and run,
Echoing giggles, oh what fun!

We compete to catch the stars that gleam,
In a dance of shadows, we gleefully beam.
A game of tag by the fading light,
Chasing as dusk turns the day to night.

Our socks are mismatched, our hair a mess,
We laugh at the chaos, we just confess.
Drawing doodles on each other's arms,
Sharing silly stories with joyful charms.

As the day bids goodbye, we share a toast,
For memories made with friends we can boast.
With echoes of happiness swirling around,
In our hearts forever, this joy we found.

Sweet Diversions in Hidden Nooks

In a garden maze, we hide and seek,
Finding laughter in every peek.
A butterfly dances, a curious friend,
As we chase our giggles, around the bend.

Candy wrappers caught in the breeze,
As we munch and munch, oh please, oh please!
With sticky fingers and faces smeared,
We devour treats, like laughter appeared.

Under the tree, where secrets lie,
We whisper dreams as birds fly by.
Silly stories make the shadows sway,
In those hidden nooks, we dreams play.

Our afternoon sparkles with whimsy bright,
Each tickle shared igniting delight.
In these sweet diversions, joy is found,
A treasure of moments that knows no bound.

Sweet Nectar of Today

The sun spills juice on the ground,
Laughter echoes all around.
With sticky hands, we chase the bee,
Life is sweet, just like the free.

A fruit fight breaks out in the park,
Someone lobbed a peach, oh what a lark!
We slip and slide on the soft grass,
Giggling hard, we let time pass.

Wipe that juice off your chin, my friend,
This moment's treasure, we won't pretend.
A picnic feast under the sun,
With silly games, our hearts have won.

As evening falls, the fruit's gone bare,
We dance and twirl without a care.
Tomorrow's promise, bright and bold,
Paints our memories, rich as gold.

Serendipity in Bloom

Stumbles turning into grace,
A custard cream spills on your face.
Laughter rings out like a bell,
Oh, what stories we can tell!

Under blooming trees we play,
Chasing shadows, banishing gray.
Caught in a game of hop and skip,
With fruit juice on our lip.

The birds join in with a joyful song,
It feels so right, nothing is wrong.
When life throws curves, we just dodge,
With every twist, our joy will lodge.

When dusk arrives, we'll gather near,
Exchanging tales, spreading cheer.
In every laugh, a little bloom,
A night of joy, dispels the gloom.

Warm Hues of Afternoon Delight

Golden rays dancing on our skin,
Silly whims turn the day to win.
A cherry pie, a slice of fun,
Who knew mischief could weigh a ton?

We roll in puddles, oh what a sight,
Splashes and giggles, pure delight.
A kite goes soaring high above,
Filled with dreams and all our love.

Mom shouts from the porch, 'Where's your hat?'
In a fruit bucket, we look like that!
Sticky fingers, and messy hair,
In our little world, we have not a care.

The sun starts to set, painting the sky,
With colors so bold, they make us sigh.
Let's bottle this joy, and keep it tight,
For tomorrow's play, and another delight.

Lush Embraces and Gentle Breezes

A gentle breeze tousles our hair,
We sneak a bite without a care.
The lawn is a stage, the world our play,
With giggles spilling, brightening the day.

We gather round with a grand old spread,
Who knew snacks could go to your head?
Chocolate stains on our shirts so bright,
We're living the dream, take flight tonight.

Under the trees, shadows waltz and sway,
Our laughter takes wings, come what may.
A silly dance in our backyard oasis,
With goofy moves, we embrace the phases.

As twilight wraps us in a warm cloak,
Beneath the stars, we giggle and poke.
For in these moments, we've found our bliss,
In every laughter, a fruity kiss.

Sunset Whispers in Warm Hues

A squirrel skipped by wearing a hat,
Chasing a sunbeam, imagine that!
The sky burst in colors, bold and bright,
While clouds played hide-and-seek with the light.

A dog dreamt of chasing a bright red ball,
While fellas on bikes took a humorous fall.
Laughter erupted, the whole park knew,
Life's bloopers are best when shared with a crew.

Butterflies danced with unsteady grace,
Even the daisies had smiles on their face.
A ticklish breeze made a few people sneeze,
While someone's ice cream took quite the tease.

As dusk softly settled, we wobbled our way,
Trading our stories to end the day.
In twilight's embrace, we laughed till we cried,
Sunset whispers, where joy cannot hide.

The Sweetness of Afternoon Light

Sunshine poured in like a fizzy drink,
Kids spun in circles, not stopping to think.
Ice cream cones stacked so high they might fall,
One lick too many and chaos for all!

A jogger tripped over his own two feet,
A comical sight in the summer heat.
Butterflies giggled with whimsical flair,
While a puppy chased shadows without a care.

Lemonade stands booming with funny jokes,
And laughter that echoed like chirping folks.
With each goofy moment, our spirits took flight,
Radiating joy in the soft afternoon light.

The sun winked at us; we waved back with glee,
As friends shared their secrets and silly decree.
In the warmth of the day, sweet antics continued,
Creating a scrapbook of funny reviewed.

Juice Dripping from Summer Smiles

A watermelon cap made the kids giggle,
Juice dripping down, they do the swizzle.
Their laughter rang loud on that sunny street,
Chasing down flavors in summer's sweet heat.

The local cat struck a pose for the show,
While ants marched on, they had places to go.
Sunscreen applied with splatters in style,
Covered in laughter, they warmed by a mile.

Picnics unfolded with sandwiches loft,
But one flew away, it took quite a scoff.
Grins turned to giggles as crumbs flew about,
Nature's a stage, there's never a doubt.

With sticky fingers and stories to share,
We danced in the sunshine without a care.
Juice dripping down but hearts open wide,
Summer smiles in a silly joyride.

Serene Days in Orchard Dreams

Orchards abound with a curious cheer,
As bees pulled their pranks buzzing close to your ear.
Children in hats climbed the tallest tree,
Trying to reach those sweet fruits carefree.

A goat stole a sandwich; it caused quite a fuss,
While birds laughed melodiously, joining us.
Kites soared high, dancing under the sky,
And each little mishap was met with a sigh.

Laughter sprinkled like petals on air,
With lemonade puddles, we didn't care.
Stories blossomed among each shady branch,
In this orchard of dreams, we took our chance.

As evening set in, we basked in delight,
Shadows grew long, hearts merry and light.
In serene little moments, we found our gleam,
Harvesting laughter in life's sweetest dream.

Cinnamon Skies and Golden Delights

In a world of laughter and juicy dreams,
We dance on the clouds, or so it seems.
With cinnamon swirls in the sunset glow,
We giggle at the antics of squirrels below.

Our friends throw fruit in a playful war,
Bananas and apples, oh, what a score!
Lemonade spills, it's a sticky affair,
But joy drips down without a care.

Every bite a chuckle, each sip a cheer,
As we toast to the moments we hold so dear.
With golden delights in the evening light,
We revel in laughter, till the stars shine bright.

A Symphony of Stone Fruits

A orchestra of cherries plays in the breeze,
As laughter rings out like new melodies.
Peaches prance in their fuzzy attire,
While plums wink at pears with mischief to inspire.

We write silly songs with bits of this and that,
With jam jars for drums, and a cat in a hat.
Apples can giggle, and oranges hum,
When life gives us lemons, we make it all fun!

In our fruit kingdom, the giggles flow,
As we tell fruit tales in the soft evening glow.
The stones get juggled; we snicker and play,
'Till the sun sets behind in a golden display.

Juicy Revelations Under the Sun

Under the sun, where the giggles reside,
We discover sweet secrets with arms open wide.
A watermelon slice is a throne fit for kings,
While oranges roll in, bringing jokes and good flings.

With laughter so loud, we forget all our cares,
Mangoes tease rhymes, while pineapple dares.
We lay in the grass, with our fruity essays,
In this sunny world, time just plays.

Every burst of flavor, a chuckle we find,
Like secrets revealed in the warmth of sunshine.
Juicy confessions that bring us delight,
Dance in the warmth, till the stars steal the light.

The Essence of a Lazy Afternoon

In hush of the afternoon, sweetness takes flight,
We lounge in the sun, with bliss in our sight.
Popcorn is glowing with a cinnamon twist,
It tickles our senses, we can't resist.

Berries roll by in a playful parade,
As we sit and debate the best way to trade.
Mismatched socks dance in the fluffy warm breeze,
While ants plot a party: Oh, look at them tease!

A half-eaten cake brings the best kind of loot,
As giggles erupt, from this fruity pursuit.
With lazy antics and full hearts we sway,
In sweet, silly moments, let's dream and play.

Embracing the Warmth of Euphoria

Sunshine spills on fuzzy skin,
Laughter dances in the breeze.
Joy bounces in the grass so green,
Tickled toes beneath tall trees.

Friends gather for a silly feast,
Sipping on that bright, sweet tea.
Chasing dreams, we're like a beast,
Finding bliss; oh, so carefree!

Chasing shadows, playing games,
The world's a stage, we're on display.
Every moment's filled with flames,
Burning bright in our own way.

When life's a riot, laugh out loud,
We wear our happiness like crowns.
In this chaos, oh so proud,
We flip our frowns and chase the downs.

Juicy Adventurers Beneath Spreading Branches

We climbed so high for fruit of gold,
Swinging down from leafy knots.
With sticky hands, our tales unfold,
We're tree-huggers; salad spots!

The juice drips down upon our chins,
Nature's gift, with laughter's touch.
Silly faces and goofy grins,
Each moment shared means so much.

We play hide-and-seek in shade,
With critters peeking, curious,
Our lazy plans seem hand-made,
Just blissful, wild, and delirious!

Splatters, spills, a sticky mess,
With laughter echoing the air.
Each bite's a burst, a happy guess,
Adventurers, without a care!

Nature's Palette of Joyful Times

Colors splash across the scene,
Nature's brush strokes bright and bold.
Every laugh, a vibrant green,
With every tale, a memory told.

Running through fields, feeling free,
Jumping puddles, splashing bright.
Dancing with bees; come join me!
The sun's a friend; it feels so right.

Canvas skies with sunset hues,
Sing for the stars, they join our song.
In this gallery of good views,
We laugh and giggle, all night long.

Skip through the woods, come take a peek,
At funny squirrels, a hoot, a wink.
Nature smiles; let's take a sneak,
At all the joy we find, we think!

Playful Touches and Fragrant Delights

Breezes kissed with floral scents,
Dancing petals whirl and twirl.
With every tickle, joy ascents,
In this wild and fragrant whirl.

Bumblebees buzzing, a gentle hum,
As colorful daisies nod in glee.
A skippy step, we're never glum,
In fields of laughter, wild and free.

A pie in the face, oh what a sight!
Creamy splats and giggles roar.
The world's a carnival tonight,
Fragrant trails lead off to more!

Marshmallow clouds up in the sky,
Melting marshmallow fluff and fun.
Each playful touch makes time fly,
In this aroma, we are one!

Dappled Light and Gentle Sighs

In the garden where giggles grow,
A bee buzzed past my nose, oh no!
With every flutter and tiny hop,
I duck and shimmy, can't let it stop.

Sunbeams dance on a sleepy cat,
Pretending she's hunting a shiny rat.
But really she's dreaming, oh what a sight,
Chasing the shadows in warm sunlight.

A picnic spread beneath a tree,
Sandwiches fly like they're free!
A squirrel snickers, snagging a chip,
Stealing my snacks with a nimble flip.

Laughter echoes, we run and chase,
Falling over in a wild embrace.
A slapstick tumble on soft green grass,
In these moments, oh how they pass!

Sun-soaked Hearts and Laughter's Echo

Splashing in puddles as raindrops fall,
My friends and I, we're having a ball.
Umbrellas flipped and laughter loud,
Soaking the day as we dance in a crowd.

Ice cream cones tipping every which way,
Chocolate drips turn to sweet ballet.
We giggle as sticky hands collide,
A sticky situation, yet we're full of pride.

Kites swirling high in a blue wide sky,
Squealing with joy as they start to fly.
One takes a dive, and oh what a scene,
Tangled in branches, it's living the dream.

Dancing in circles, round and round,
Falling over, smack on the ground.
We laugh till it hurts, the moments we miss,
In this sun-soaked joy, we find our bliss!

Vibrant Fables of Summer's Bliss

Bubbles floating, drifting high,
In a race with a butterfly up in the sky.
A burst of giggles fills the air,
As dogs chase tails without a care.

Water balloons create a splash,
Launching at friends—a colorful bash.
Shrieks and chuckles as we all run,
A blurry mess, but oh, what fun!

Barbecues sizzling with a smoky song,
Grill masters flipping—who could go wrong?
A bit too charred, the burgers are black,
Yet everyone eats, there's no holding back.

Starry nights with a campfire glow,
Telling tall tales, oh what a show!
Marshmallow wars with sticky sweet aim,
In vibrant fables, we fuel the flame!

Radiant Laughter that Blossoms

In fields of daisies, we skip and twirl,
With crowns of flowers, we dance and whirl.
A ladybug lands upon my nose,
I sneeze and giggle at how it goes.

Chasing tiny frogs in a sunlit pond,
Their jumps are funny, I'm truly conned!
With each high leap, my laugh grows loud,
A froggy spring in our playful crowd.

Fall in a pile of leaves so bright,
A rustling symphony, what pure delight!
We hide and seek in nature's embrace,
With each silly step, we quicken the pace.

As day turns to night, stars gleam above,
We share our secrets, our dreams, our love.
In radiant joy, we find our way,
Each laughter blossoms with every play!

Golden Echoes of Blissful Routes

On a bicycle built for two,
We wobbled, giggled, and flew.
The ice cream fell, oh what a sight,
Sticky hands turned the world bright.

A dog chased us, tail all aflame,
Barking loudly, like it's a game.
We laughed so hard, we lost our way,
Maps forgotten, who needs to pay?

Sunshine danced on the cobbled stone,
With every bump, we felt less alone.
A honking car, what a surprise,
We turned and waved, laughed till we cried.

Oh the bliss, like bubbles in air,
With laughter echoing everywhere.
Every moment, a joyful tease,
In the spirit of adventure, we freeze.

Splashes of Warmth on Blissful Days

A splash of water, laughter begins,
Down the slide, where everyone spins.
Sunscreen's slathered, in crusty layers,
We're the champions of goofy prayers.

Friends in the pool, with antics galore,
Cannonballs flying, we laugh and roar.
Floating a raft, with snacks piled high,
Beeching a seagull, oh my, oh my!

A water balloon, a sneaky toss,
Splattering Jason, oh what a loss!
He flails and flops, an angel indeed,
We rise in giggles, fulfilling the need.

As sun tucks in for a glowing night,
We gather 'round, sharing all the delight.
Every splash, a moment divine,
Full of warmth, under the stars we shine.

Forgotten Secrets in Sunny Clefs

A tune on the ukulele, off key but bright,
Singing together, with all our might.
In a park so green, where shadows play,
Each note a secret, from yesterday.

A lost flip-flop, the crime of the day,
While squirrels dive in, with stolen hay.
We dance in circles, oh what a mess,
Tripping in laughter, we couldn't care less.

The sun peeks cheeky, through fluffy clouds,
Winking at us, as we sing loud.
Each chord a giggle, a burst of joy,
Like children again, with our favorite toy.

As petals flutter, a gentle breeze,
We find forgotten secrets, if you please.
In this sunny clef, where hearts entwine,
Laughter weaves tales, oh how they shine.

The Melody of Joyful Confections

Candy stores glow, with colorful sweets,
A sugar rush dance, where laughter meets.
Chocolate fountains, a splashy delight,
We drench our faces, oh what a sight!

Jellybeans bounce, like they're on a quest,
Every nibble is like a fun fest.
Cupcakes toppled, frosting in hair,
Mocking each other, who's got the flair?

Licorice sticks, we spin like a top,
Our playful spirits, they never stop.
Giggling and snorting, we share our stash,
Every sweet bite turns friendship to cash.

As daydreams linger, the sun fades slow,
With pockets of candy, our laughter will glow.
In this melody, flavors collide,
Together we savor the moments, side by side.

Orchard Secrets and Sugary Smiles

In the orchard, secrets hide,
Where fruits giggle and confide.
A squirrel snickers, chasing a bee,
While I trip over roots, laughing with glee.

Sunshine dapples the leaves so bright,
As I mash berries, what a sight!
Sticky fingers and sugar high,
My friends agree, it's worth a try!

Lemonade spills, a fizzy delight,
We dance and slip, oh what a fright!
But laughter echoes through the day,
Each silly moment just fades away.

We pluck the fruit with silly styles,
Caught in the giggles, it's worth the miles.
Orchard dreams with friends in tow,
Sugary smiles, in summer's glow.

Sunlit Petals on a Warm Breeze

Sunlit petals flutter in the air,
We twirl like leaves without a care.
A gust of wind, our hats take flight,
Chasing them down brings pure delight.

Dandelions dance, becoming our crowns,
Reigning over fields, king and clowns.
Giggles erupt from a stumble,
As we fall down and start to rumble.

Butterflies join in the hilarious race,
Painting our faces in a joyful embrace.
Each step is lighter, laughter spills free,
Nature chuckles, come join the spree!

Breezes whisper secrets so grand,
We skip and hop, hand in hand.
Sunlit days with friends so dear,
In flowery chaos, we shed a tear.

Vibrant Hues of Joyful Chaos

Crayons scattered in vibrant hues,
We scribble on clouds and wear our shoes.
A splash of paint, a giggle so loud,
Artistic disasters make us feel proud.

With every color, chaos ignites,
We paint our neighbors and call it delights.
Splatters of orange grace the tree,
As we run from laughter, wild and free.

A canvas of grass turns tie-dye green,
With every wrong step, we reign supreme.
Our playful mess, a masterpiece still,
In the rambunctious thrills, we find our thrill.

Laughter echoes as colors collide,
In joyful chaos, we take pride.
Each stroke is a moment, wild and loud,
Vibrant hues, amidst the crowd!

Nectar Dripping from Laughing Lips

Sweet nectar drips from laughing lips,
As we feast on fruit, delight in sips.
A watermelon slice, laughter's embrace,
We juice up our cheeks, each funny face.

Sticky fingers reach for more,
A jolly tug-of-war on the floor.
Banana peels lead to a slide,
As we tumble and giggle, no need to hide.

Juicy berries burst with glee,
Messy munchers, happy as can be.
Fruits in the air, let laughter fly,
In this fruity world, we'll never shy.

With each sugary laugh, hearts collide,
Honey-sweet moments we cannot hide.
Nectar on lips, giggles abound,
In this joyful paradise, love is found.

Fragrant Journeys Through Orchard Dreams

In orchards bright with fruit so sweet,
I stumbled on a yellow seat.
A squirrel joined me, quite a sight,
To share his stash and take a bite.

With every crunch, the juice would spray,
He laughed and danced, oh what a play!
I told a joke, he rolled his eyes,
Then tossed an acorn, oh what a prize!

We chatted 'bout the trees and bees,
While swatting at some hungry fleas.
He claimed he'd run a fruiting race,
But tripped and fell, what a disgrace!

As sunlight waned, we bid adieu,
My furry friend, with a jaunty view.
In colorful shades, our laughter soared,
In dreams of fruit, we both adored.

Golden Hours and Honeyed Smiles

Once there was a chef so bold,
He baked with fruits of red and gold.
His muffins flopped, they fell like bricks,
He shrugged, then threw in extra tricks.

With honey drizzled, they looked divine,
But tasted more like sour brine.
His friends all cheered, with dubious grins,
"Next time, mate, do stick to skins!"

A picnic planned, all set to feast,
With laughter rising, joy increased.
But ants declared it their domain,
And soon the table, was quite a gain.

Yet golden hours still found a way,
With honeyed smiles that made our day.
We laughed so hard, we nearly cried,
In fruit-filled fun, we all abide.

Blissful Bites of Summer's Essence

A watermelon, oh what a prize,
I sliced it thin, to much surprise.
My dog, by chance, took quite a leap,
And landed with a mighty beep!

We shared a slice, juicy and red,
While drips and giggles filled our spread.
His fur was sticky, oh what a sight,
As bees buzzed in with pure delight.

Then came a peach, shiny and round,
It slipped right out, fell on the ground.
We chased it down, a comical race,
And both went splat, what a silly face!

Yet blissful bites made us forgive,
With every munch, we truly live.
In summer's glow, our laughter grew,
With fruity fun in all we do.

Radiance in Every Lifelike Bite

In my kitchen, chaos reigns supreme,
With fruits and veggies, forming a team.
I tried to cook, with flair and grace,
But ended up in quite the race.

My blender whirred with wild delight,
Onions flew, oh what a sight!
A carrot bounced, right off my shoe,
"A dance party!" yelled my friend, "Woo-hoo!"

With every bite, a colorful mess,
We laughed so hard, we lost our stress.
A salad gone rogue, a splatter galore,
Made memories found, forevermore.

Yet amidst the giggles and cheerful cheer,
We feasted like royalty, no time for fear.
For radiance glowed in every bite,
In lively feasts, we found our light.

Threads of Joy Interwoven in Light

In the garden, socks on our heads,
Laughter bounces, where humor spreads.
Butterflies dance, with silly glee,
Tickling flowers, come join our spree.

Sunshine giggles, hiding in trees,
Chasing shadows, a game of tease.
With each stitch of laughter we weave,
Threads of joy in our hearts, we believe.

Frogs in bow ties, they leap and croon,
While we sway to a playful tune.
Oh, what a sight, the world so bright,
In this moment, all feels just right.

So let's paint the skies with colors bold,
Life's silly stories are sweet to be told.
With a wink and a smile, let worries take flight,
As we dance in the threads of pure delight.

Blossoming Joy in Nature's Embrace

In a field where daisies wear hats,
We giggle and skip, oh how time chats!
Bunnies with glasses, playing charades,
Join us in laughter, let worries fade.

The trees sway like they know a joke,
Their branches wave, and the sunlight pokes.
With clouds that flaunt their fluffy tricks,
Nature offers joy that always sticks.

Squirrels in capes, on daring flights,
Stealing our snacks with humorous bites.
Each breeze carries laughter, light, and free,
In this embrace, we eternal glee.

So let's frolic where silly reigns,
Sprinkling joy like a summer rain.
Every petal and leaf sings our tune,
In this dance, we're forever immune.

Sweet Simplicity Among the Leaves

With leaves that chuckle, whispers so sweet,
We wander the woods, with funny feet.
A raccoon in sneakers, oh what a sight,
Stealing our snacks in the broad daylight!

The sun tickles trees, a playful tease,
Rustling leaves say, "Let's do as we please!"
A squirrel juggles acorns, round and round,
In the symphony of joy, laughter is found.

The brook winks at us, with stories to share,
While butterflies giggle in warm summer air.
Each moment a gift, wrapped in delight,
In this simple bliss, our hearts take flight.

Among the leaves, our laughter springs,
With light hearts, we dance while the forest sings.
In the sweet simplicity, we'll always weave,
Memories of laughter, we'll never leave.

Fragrant Whispers Lost in Serenity

In a field of blooms, we spin and twirl,
Honeybees buzz, in our laughter, they swirl.
A dog in a hat, with a cheeky grin,
Shares a giggle, where joy can begin.

The breeze tells secrets; we lean in close,
Tickled by petals, we cheer and we boast.
With flowers that dance, like they know the score,
Our hearts grow light, as we twirl on the floor.

The clouds make faces, soft as a sigh,
While grasshoppers practice their leap to the sky.
In this moment, where silliness reigns,
We gather the laughter like soft, gentle rains.

So come join our fun in this fragrant space,
Where whims take flight at a joyful pace.
In the whispers of nature, we find our way,
Lost in the moment, we laugh and we play.

Sweet Respite Beneath the Canopy

In the shade where giggles play,
Bees are buzzing, come what may.
Sandwiches dance, crumbs take flight,
As ants march in, a quirky sight.

Lemonade spills, a sunny shower,
Laughter blooms like a bright flower.
We chase our dreams on a blanket spread,
With silly hats atop our heads.

Giant leaves, our sun-kissed shade,
We argue if it's homemade or trade.
Tickling toes while the world skips,
Each moment savored, in hearty sips.

Under the branches, stories flow,
A hiccup, a snort, laughter's glow.
We're all a bit nutty, no need to explain,
In our secret garden of joy and refrain.

Sunkissed Invitations to Blissful Days

The sun peeks in with its golden grin,
We dart outside, let the games begin.
With ice cream smiles and sticky hands,
We leap like frogs over sunlit sands.

Bubbles float, a sheer delight,
Popping each other's dreams with all our might.
Hot dogs twist in a playful dance,
As laughter swirls, we seize the chance.

A picnic blanket, patchwork charm,
Mosquitoes buzz— oh, what a harm!
But we swat them with delight and grace,
While savoring ketchup on our face.

Sunkissed we sit, an odd little crew,
With mismatched socks and a wayward shoe.
Time drips sweet, an endless play,
As silly stories take us away.

Golden Sun-Kissed Whispers

Golden rays tease the wiggle of toes,
Chasing shadows where the wild grass grows.
Whispers of mischief swirl in the breeze,
As we plot our next great escapade with ease.

Grass stains and giggles, we tumble and fall,
A frisbee flies, just miss the wall!
We're all a little clumsy, but who really cares?
We're kings and queens of these soft, grassy lairs.

In a sun-dappled glen, we set up shop,
With lemonade glasses and a croquet top.
Birds chirp along, a concert for free,
While we compete in our own candy spree.

The day drips sweet, like honey in tea,
With every laugh, we barely can see.
Laughter escapes like a bubbly stream,
As we craft our fortress of ice cream dreams.

Juicy Laughter Under Sunny Skies

Juicy fruits roll around our feet,
As we race to collect each tasty treat.
Sticky fingers splash in delight,
Gulping down goodness, oh what a sight!

Sipping smoothies, we share our tales,
Of superheroes, slip-ups, and epic fails.
Sunshine wraps us in a warm embrace,
While we pull silly faces without a trace.

Picnic chaos as ants convene,
A fruit salad battle, oh what a scene!
We toast with berries, our laughter entwined,
In these sunny moments, joy's all we find.

With clouds like whipped cream drifting near,
We bask in the glow, nothing to fear.
As the sun bids farewell with a wink,
We chuckle and sigh, a sweet moment to think.

Cheerful Reflections in Ripe Shadows

In the garden where giggles play,
Sunlight dances, bright like a ballet.
The fruit hangs low with a wink so sly,
Buzzing bees join in, oh my, oh my!

Laughter bursts like bubbles in air,
Every silly moment without a care.
We chase the shadows, we skip and twirl,
Life's a comedy, give it a whirl!

Sticky fingers reach for delight,
Jam on toast, oh what a sight!
With silly hats and ice-cream spills,
Our laughter echoes over the hills!

Dreams float by on cotton candy clouds,
Welcoming giggles in merry crowds.
In every bite, a chuckle we find,
The sweetest laughter, oh joy unconfined!

Moments that Melt Like Warm Honey

Who needs plans when fun's in the air?
Golden rays sneak into my hair.
A drizzle of syrup, a splash of cheer,
Every moment ripe, perfect, and clear.

The world spins 'round in a whirl of glee,
Silly dances, just you and me.
With jellybeans spilled, we race for the prize,
Oh look, a piñata – what a surprise!

Warm rays slide down our cheeky grin,
Tickling toes as the fun begins.
Laughter whirls like firefly lights,
In this honey dream, we soar to new heights!

With sticky fingers and a fully bloomed heart,
Each moment of sweetness, a joyful art.
Sunshine giggles like it's on a spree,
What a wild world of sweet jubilee!

The Sweetness of Now and Always

A little chaos mixed with bright sun,
Every awkward moment - oh, how they run!
Smiles in a fruit basket, ripe and round,
Every ticklish joke, oh so profound!

In the kitchen, a flour fight breaks,
Cake batter splashes, oh what mistakes!
With spoons as microphones, we sing along,
In this home of giggles, we all belong.

Life's a pie sliced with cherry delight,
Even the burnt bits shine oh so bright.
The flavor of laughter, joy on display,
Every bite of happiness here to stay!

With snapshots and laughter, we aim for the sky,
Serendipitous moments, better than pie.
Let's freeze these seconds in honeyed embrace,
For smiles and chuckles, there's always a place!

Honeyed Breezes and Luminous Days

Whirling leaves dance in honeyed air,
Giggling children without a care.
Sunshine breezes tickle our skin,
As hugs and laughter together begin.

A splash of color in the open field,
The joy of nature is our shield.
Chasing rainbows, we stumble and fall,
Laughter erupts, we're having a ball!

Silly dances at the picnic spread,
With watermelons as our feast ahead.
Spinning tales like a sweet summer breeze,
Every moment cherished, oh, if you please!

Honey drips from time's gentle hand,
Crafting memories in this golden land.
So here's to laughter, and all that we share,
In luminous days, let's play without care!

An Evening Bathed in Ripe Delight

A squirrel wore my hat, oh what a sight,
Chasing its tail in the fading light.
Laughter spilled like juice from a split can,
As friends joined in, forming a silly clan.

We danced with shadows, our feet in a swirl,
While a rogue breeze made our hair curl.
With splashes of laughter, we painted the sky,
In a symphony of giggles, oh my, oh my!

Tossing sticky snacks like confetti in air,
Each bite a surprise, with a fruit-flavored flare.
The sunset smiled, making the moment grand,
As we plopped down, making messes unplanned.

Under the glow of a fading sunbeam,
All the whispers turned into a dream.
We toasted to fun, in our quirky way,
Savoring the joy of this goofy play.

The Echo of Sunswept Laughter

Chasing each other through fields of gold,
With secret giggles, stories unfold.
A game of tag turned into a chase,
As we all raced with glee, it was pure embrace.

The dog joined in, a furry whirlwind,
Knocking over the snacks, we couldn't rescind.
Belly laughs echoed on this sunny day,
As spills and thrills led us all astray.

We wore fruit hats made from scraps we found,
Crowning our heads, we danced round and round.
With every wobble and silly little leap,
Our hearts were light, with memories to keep.

The sun dipped down, but laughter stayed bright,
Happiness painted the coming night.
As we collapsed in a heap, our cheeks all aglow,
In the echo of giggles, our joy stole the show.

Bursting with Joy Under Open Skies

A picnic spread under the sky so blue,
Filled with treasures, like cakes, who knew?
But as we dove in, ants crashed the feast,
Though we squealed and laughed, they came in increased.

We wore napkins like capes, feeling like kings,
Dodging each other, oh what funny things!
With sandwiches flung like frisbees in space,
Food fights erupted, oh what a disgrace!

The watermelon splats formed a fruity art,
Splashing colors, a masterpiece from the start.
As juice dripped down our chins like a trick,
We burst into laughter—oh, that was the kick!

The breeze played tunes, whispering so sweet,
Filling our souls with this whimsical treat.
Under open skies where nonsense holds sway,
We embraced every giggle, come what may.

Gathering Warmth in Vibrant Pockets

In jackets too big, we bundled up tight,
Huddled together, sharing pure light.
Telling tall tales with exaggerated flair,
While laughter erupted—oh how we'd dare!

Pockets were filled with treasure galore,
Candy and giggles, who could ask for more?
We swapped silly secrets, our faces aglow,
In the warmth of the moment, we let our joy flow.

A contest of voices to see who could squeak,
Cracking us up, making laughter peak.
High-fives exchanged with each funny line,
As we tumbled and rolled, feeling so fine.

And when the world turned a shimmering gray,
We found our warmth in the games we played.
With vibrant pockets and hearts full of cheer,
In our bubble of joy, we conquered all fear.

Golden Threads of Delightful Whimsy

In the park, a duck does dance,
Waddling in a silly trance.
Children giggle, pointing fast,
A game of tag, a perfect blast.

Kites are flying, colors bright,
Tangled strings, oh what a sight!
One brave soul lets out a shout,
"Who's the hero?" No one's out!

Ice cream drips on sunny days,
Sticky fingers, laughter plays.
Crispy treats at every bend,
Sharing joy, you can't pretend.

Silly hats atop our heads,
Giggles burst like couch-bound spreads.
We'll recall these moments spent,
Where every laugh was time well lent.

Serenades of Warmth and Light

Balloons that fly in evening glow,
Frogs make sounds, a quirky show.
Dance around with silly grace,
While rubber chickens join the chase.

A sunbeam tickles the picnic spread,
Sandwich fights, with crumbs we're fed.
Mischief blends with golden rays,
Tickling toes in playful ways.

Butterflies flutter with delight,
Chasing shadows, taking flight.
A stray dog joins the happy throng,
In this moment, we all belong.

With laughter echoing through the air,
Everyone knows, we have no care.
A party of joy beneath the sun,
Together, always, we have fun!

Savoring the Essence of Laughter

Coffee spills in morning glee,
Laughter rings, oh that's the key!
Cream and sugar, what a mix,
Stirring up our playful tricks.

Board games stacked in disarray,
Someone's losing, but hey, who's sway?
Funny faces, the bets are on,
With every roll, our cares are gone.

Silly stories shared at night,
Under the stars, such pure delight.
One last joke, let's take a chance,
Breaking into a wild dance.

With every giggle, bonds grow strong,
In this tale, we all belong.
Let's savor each uproarious spree,
In laughter's arms, we're wild and free.

Sweet Hues of Resplendent Days

Bubbles floating in the breeze,
Chasing rainbows with such ease.
Giggles spill with every pop,
Sweet delight, we can't quite stop.

Candy sticks and treats galore,
Sticky fingers, we ask for more.
Each sweet bite brings forth a cheer,
Laughter rings, we hold it dear.

Chalk drawings on sidewalks bright,
Jumping puddles, pure delight.
Whimsical worlds, we create and play,
In our hearts, they'll always stay.

As the sun dips low at dusk,
Memories bloom, an endless husk.
Days that shimmer, filled with cheer,
Forever captured, held so near.

Sun-Kissed Adventures Awaiting

The sun beams down with a wink,
Laughter echoes, sweet as a drink.
Chasing shadows, we play all day,
In the warmth of gold, we dance and sway.

A picnic planned with treats galore,
Mismatched socks and silly lore.
Ice cream drips on our sunny cheeks,
Joyful giggles, the kind that peaks.

Feet in the grass, we smile and strain,
Swatting flies like a wild campaign.
With each sip of soda, bubbles fly,
In this silly fest, oh me, oh my!

Adventure calls, with a playful lure,
Chasing each other, hearts so pure.
In every moment, carefree and bright,
We relish laughter, from morn till night.

The Flavor of Happiness in Every Slice

Slices served on a paper plate,
Juicy morsels that simply await.
With every bite, a giggle spills,
Fruits collide, creating thrills.

Lemonade stands and sticky hands,
Chasing flavors across the sands.
A picnic basket filled to the brim,
With laughter and joy, we sing and grin.

Pineapple hats and watermelon crowns,
Dancing around in vibrant gowns.
Each slice shared brings a silly quirk,
Underneath sunflowers, we play and smirk.

From zestful bites to fruity spills,
Life is a laugh with all its frills.
When sweetness mingles with a wink,
Every moment makes our hearts blink.

Harmonies of Juice and Laughter

Bubbly drinks in colorful cups,
With laughter flowing, we can't get enough.
Sipping joy under the sun's glow,
Friends together, letting time flow.

Splatters of juice, a fun little fight,
As fruit confetti fills the light.
With every chuckle, we toast a cheer,
This silly fest, oh, we hold dear.

Tunes of summer drift through the air,
As dancing feet embrace without a care.
Lemon slices in our funny hats,
Joy in abundance, and that's that!

With every sip, a new joke lands,
We raise our glasses with silly hands.
Cheers to the moments where laughs ignite,
With juice and joy, we own the night.

Sun-Soaked Moments of Simple Bliss

Golden rays warm our happy faces,
Chasing sunshine in our favorite places.
With silly poses, we strike a pose,
In sun-kissed fields, anything goes.

Sunflowers dance, they sway and twirl,
A day of fun, let the laughter unfurl.
A shade of mischief in our blissful sighs,
As the soft breeze carries joyful cries.

Kites fly high, yet we tumble and trip,
With giggles and grins from each little slip.
Ice cream flavors that swirl and mix,
In summer chaos, it's pure magic tricks.

With every sunset, our spirits take flight,
Thankful for days that feel just right.
In the warmth of each sun-soaked kiss,
We find life's joy in little bliss.

A Basket Overflowing with Joy

In a field of laughter, we skip and play,
With sun-kissed cheeks, we chase the day.
Mismatched socks and a shoe on the tree,
Life's little blunders, oh, how fun to see!

A pie in the face, what a delightful scene,
Whipped cream giggles, we're all so serene.
Chasing our dreams on a whimsy ride,
Through tangled gardens, we laugh and glide.

A dance with the bees, oh what a sight,
Twisting and swirling, we dance in delight.
Tangled in joy, let the good times roll,
Every little mishap, a story to toll.

With friends by our side, all worries erased,
We're a slapstick crew, leaving humor traced.
From spilled drinks to jokes that don't land,
Life's a buffet, we take it unplanned.

Honeyed Breezes and Soft Embraces

Breezy whispers tickle our ears,
While laughter bubbles, washing away fears.
Kites in the air, we run with delight,
Chasing the clouds in a giggly flight.

Lemonade sipping while we squirt and splash,
Oh, the joy found in a simple crash.
Sticky fingers reach for candy galore,
Sweet discoveries waiting behind every door.

Fluffy rabbits and butterflies flutter,
In a whimsical world where our hearts start to stutter.
Silly tales spin in the golden sun,
In this fateful play, we're all together fun.

Soft embraces melt like ice cream cones,
As we giggle and wiggle, forgetting our phones.
Together we sway in nature's sweet grace,
In a tapestry woven, laughter leaves a trace.

The Lush Tapestry of Summer Days

Sunshine pouring like syrupy gold,
In dandelion dreams, magic unfolds.
Brushing off ants from our picnic spread,
With sandwiches flying, all stomachs are fed.

A jump in the pool, but wait! What a splash,
Cannonballs echo with laughter so brash.
Napping in hammocks as breezes pass by,
Floating on clouds in a soft, painted sky.

Popsicle drips on our sun-kissed skin,
Bubbles and giggles, let the fun begin!
Crazy hats on our heads, we strike a pose,
In this quirky dance, anything goes.

With tree-climbing heroes scaling the heights,
And missing the mark in our kitchen flights.
Each afternoon's treasure, a story to tell,
In the lush summer whispers, we giggle so well.

Spilled Secrets and Sweet Emotions

Whispers of dreams in the twilight's embrace,
Stumbling on secrets, we laugh in this space.
Over spilled juice and a hiccuped cheer,
Funny expressions lead to grins ear to ear.

A treasure hunt lost on a muddled path,
With mismatched clues causing all kinds of wrath.
We weave tales so silly, they catch us by storm,
In our laughter-filled castle, we break every norm.

With confetti in pockets and cake on our face,
Every mishap becomes part of our race.
Flipping our jokes like a pancake delight,
In this cozy chaos, our hearts feel so light.

From gummy bears swapped to a friendship so grand,
We share in this mess, hand in sticky hand.
Moments like these, where the quirks come alive,
In our joyful embrace, together we thrive.

www.ingramcontent.com/pod-product-compliance
Lightning Source LLC
Chambersburg PA
CBHW070314120526
44590CB00017B/2675